IRS
WAR STORIES

IRS
WAR STORIES

Real People, Real Stories,
Real Struggles With the IRS
Volume 1

CHRIS MICKLATCHER

IRS War Stories - Volume 1
Copyright © 2017-2018 Christopher J. Micklatcher.

LIABILITY DISCLAIMER

CONTACT INFO
FRESH START TAX SOLUTIONS
510 Columbia Avenue East
Battle Creek, Michigan 49014
1-269-969-9752
http://freshstarttaxsolutions.com

GOT QUESTIONS? NEED HELP?

In this book, I hope you'll discover that your particular tax problem is not unique to just you. Others…millions of others…have faced the same problem. You are not alone.

Look around at work or in the store. Statistics show that one out of seven Americans have some sort of tax problem. You are not alone.

My goal is to have you call a tax professional before it gets worse. Don't wait until the IRS levies your paycheck or bank account. Don't wait until you panic, and call some "800 number" tax resolution firm. There is a tax professional near you, and they can help turn your life around.

We dedicate our time and energy to helping individuals and businesses through the IRS maze. Like my current and former clients, it's time you get your life back too.

The wilderness you find yourself in is simply the road between the wreckage of the past and the life you want to lead.
You only need to stop and ask for directions.
–Chris Micklatcher

For more information, go to
http://freshstarttaxsolutions.com
or call 1-269-969-9752

TABLE OF CONTENTS

ACKNOWLEDGEMENTS

The author gratefully acknowledges the following people for their support and contributions:

My wife, Nancy, my biggest supporter, cheerleader and muse, who edited my manuscript and picked up the slack for our family while I wrote this book.

My many mentors who have shaped my understanding and appreciation of tax resolution, including, Attorney Robert McKenzie, CPA Larry Lawler, and Michael Rozbruch. The list is really much longer than this!

The thousands of clients who have entrusted me with the tax issues throughout the thirty plus years I have practiced tax law. I've learned as much from them as they have from me.

INTRODUCTION

Hello. My name is Chris Micklatcher. I'm a Michigan attorney and certified public accountant and have worked to resolve taxpayer problems since 1991. I'm an old-timer, and I have seen the good, bad and ugly tax cases.

This book is written to let you know that you're not the only one who has faced the wrath of the IRS, and that there is a way out.

The stories inside this book are a compilation of just a few cases that stick out in my mind. I don't discuss in great detail the particular methods we use to resolve the cases, but rather want you to realize that others struggle with the IRS just as you do. Names and places have been changed to protect the identity of my clients.

I also don't explain step-by-step instructions on how to get relief from the crushing weight of the IRS. There are plenty of books that *try* to do that.

My recommendation has always been to find a local, competent tax professional to help you. Don't panic and call the next "800 number" tax resolution firm you hear on the radio or see on the television. There is local help available. In the last chapter of this book, I give you information on how to find a local professional.

So, enjoy the book. Maybe you'll find your story inside these pages.

CHAPTER 1
PRIORITIES

Hernando:
Portland, Maine

Hernando was one of my first clients. Thinking back, this case was resolved over twenty years ago.

Hernando's tax nightmare did not happen overnight. It was five years in the making. Hernando found me through the phone book when he had just turned twenty five years old. He was smart, and obviously a very hard worker. But he owed taxes, and the IRS was after him.

The real story with Hernando is that he was raising his four siblings. Both of his parents were gone.

It's safe to say that Hernando was the son that any parent would be proud of.

His parents immigrated to America. From Hernando's description, they had been living the American dream in earlier years. They met in Portland, Maine, got engaged, and were married soon after Hernando was born. Ten years later his parents decided to have more children, and Hernando suddenly became the big brother to four.

The extra mouths to feed took a toll on the family. While Hernando was doing well in high school and had earned a scholarship to the local college, his father began to drink heavily. Soon, he was gone from their lives.

By then Hernando left to attend college and, in addition to the little government aid they received, his mother worked as a cleaning lady to make ends meet.

While in his second year of college Hernando's mother died suddenly. Now both parents were gone, and Hernando was left with four young siblings.

Hernando left college to raise his four young siblings. He got a job at a local grocery store chain and quickly moved into management. With his paycheck, all the needs of the family were met. His siblings were now in high school and did not need as much supervision, so Hernando took a second night job at a local card shop. He was now able to provide his siblings the "extras." He wanted his siblings to be able to enjoy extracurricular activities his parents never had the money for when he was young.

But Hernando had a secret. Hernando was not paying his taxes. When Hernando first came home to take care of his siblings, he claimed thirteen dependents on his employer tax forms so that less taxes were withheld. He needed the extra cash flow to pay the bills, but now he was making very good money and he owed taxes. In fact, he owed a lot of taxes.

Over a three to five-year period, he owed about thirty-six thousand dollars including interest and penalties. This was a huge problem he had avoided. Until now.

Due to Hernando's failure to contact the IRS even after they sent countless letters, they levied his paycheck.

His employer handed him the levy notice a week earlier, and he was told that his paycheck would be continuously levied until the IRS debt was paid off in full. He would be left with about one-quarter of his regular paycheck.

What would this do to the family now? Hernando did not know. The youngest sibling was still in middle school. Though the family had moved several times over the years, Hernando simply wanted to provide a stable home until his brothers and sisters were out of school. This was not going to happen now.

When Hernando received the levy notice from his employer, he called the IRS. He tried to talk reasonably to them, but he quickly found that was not the right approach to take with the strongest, most brutal collection agency in the world.

Hernando ended up in my office a few days later.

We talked for close to an hour, and I started to gather his financial information.

Due to the fact Hernando did not contact me earlier, I could not immediately stop the levy. The employer had already received the letter, and payday was the day before. But before the second levy I was able to collect more detailed information. This allowed me to contact the IRS with a proposed action plan. We started to get some traction.

After hours of talking to the IRS revenue officer, it became clear we would not come up with a solution to pay the amount of the tax liability in full. It was obvious that if

Hernando paid what taxes he owed each month, he would have a hard time paying his current household bills.

So, what did we do?

I was able to convince the IRS that Hernando could not pay them anything at all. In fact, as a result of the IRS levy, his family would be unable to pay the rent. Hernando was in a hardship situation. As a result, the IRS made Hernando currently not collectible, or CNC. The IRS released the levy as long as Hernando agreed to adjust his withholdings so that he did not owe on his income tax return going forward. We agreed.

The levy was released.

Now, for the rest of the story.

Hernando would never be able to pay such a large debt to the IRS. Though the IRS did not send levy notices to him, three years later the debt had grown to nearly fifty thousand dollars. The nightmare was not going away and hung over Hernando like a bad dream.

But we had a plan. In very limited circumstances, you can file bankruptcy and have your income taxes discharged altogether. We did just that. After filing, the IRS discharged Alex's back taxes and he was able to get on with his life raising his siblings.

This was a tough case that lasted several years until Hernando was able to file bankruptcy with the IRS. We were successful! A fifty thousand dollar IRS tax debt reduced to less than one thousand dollars!

But that success is not what I remember about this young man. Hernando was one of my first cases, and when he walked into my life he was hurting. But because he trusted me to direct him through the maze of IRS rules and regulations, he was able to get his life back. This case was a life changing event for me, and propelled me from managing a general law and accounting firm to focusing more time and effort in resolving tax problems for individuals and businesses.

CHAPTER 2
BETRAYAL

Susan:
Grand Rapids, Michigan

Susan was married to her high school sweetheart and, by all appearances, had a happy marriage that produced three children. Her husband owned his own business in the construction industry, and he had several crews working for him. The family lived in a gated community, belonged to the local country club, and had the ability to help out family members in need. It was a charmed life…or was it?

Her husband's success apparently went to his head, and he needed to finance his growing business. He convinced Susan to get a large line of credit on the house. But he was not financing his business. He had to pay off gambling debts and finance his drug and alcohol addiction. And her husband did not stop there. He sold his business receivables to continue financing his habits.

The IRS was visiting the house regularly to talk with her husband about unpaid payroll taxes on the business. They would only talk to him about the business taxes, and he was rarely home.

Susan's charmed life was turning into a nightmare.

As this progressed, Susan's husband failed to come home for days on end, living in local hotels and charging his lifestyle to the family credit cards.

Susan felt scared and alone. She could take it no longer, and wanted out. Facing her worse fears, she filed for divorce.

The only asset left in the marriage, it seemed, was the house. She thought the house had some equity that could be used to start a new life. In the divorce her husband gladly gave it to her, and she felt some relief as she got a financial life raft in this sinking ship of a marriage. To her disappointment, she learned the house line-of-credit had eaten a large part of the equity, but she wanted the remainder nonetheless. Something was better than nothing.

In the divorce decree, her husband agreed to pay off the house line-of-credit in full. Now Susan could sell the house and use the proceeds to start a new life with her two school aged children. Victory!! Or was it?

Then came another betrayal. Her ex-husband immediately filed bankruptcy after the divorce. He was never planning to pay off the IRS or the mortgage!

Now Susan was left with a house with a large mortgage and an IRS tax lien related to her husband's unpaid employment taxes. There was no equity left. She would start her new life with nothing from her twenty five years of marriage.

Susan and her children moved into an apartment building in the same school district. The children were angry at their father's betrayal of the family, and Susan spent more time than a parent should ever be expected to, comforting them. She still needed to pay the bills, so she soon started a job cleaning an office building at night.

The house was foreclosed upon, and any remaining equity went to the IRS to pay her ex-husband's old payroll tax liabilities that were secured by the house. Susan's ex-husband may not have owned the house after the divorce, but the tax lien was filed before the divorce and was enforceable against the new owner…Susan. She received nothing.

What came next was crushing. When Susan sold the house she had capital gains, and she owed taxes. But she did not know this. Susan filed the tax return herself, never considering the house sale as income because she did not receive any proceeds from the sale.

The house sold for seven hundred thousand dollars, and while the first two hundred and fifty thousand were tax-free, she owed taxes on the remainder. Normally she could have reduced the gain by the cost of the house, but her husband had those records and he could not be found. Just when she thought she was done with the IRS and the State of Michigan, she now faced a new tax liability that only she was responsible for.

Her tax liability was over one hundred twenty thousand dollars to the IRS, and five thousand dollars to the State of Michigan. And this was just from the sale of the house.

Susan was referred to my office by a friend who knew we resolved tax debts, and we talked. She did not know where to turn, but needed answers quickly because the State of Michigan Tax Collection Department threatened to levy her small paycheck.

Why would they threaten to levy for a five thousand tax debt that was from a tax return less than a year old? We found out. Her ex-husband had not paid taxes to the IRS nor State of Michigan for previous years either. In fact, there were previous years involved which Susan thought were paid and were never disclosed in the divorce. Since her ex-husband filed bankruptcy, he was no longer responsible and the State of Michigan was coming after her for another ten thousand dollars in addition to the five thousand already owed on the sale of the house. Simply put, the State was aggressive because they lost out on any proceeds from the house, which the IRS received.

Now our office knew about two tax liabilities that Susan was solely responsible for. They totaled about two hundred thousand dollars to the IRS, and about fifteen thousand dollars to the State of Michigan.

After reviewing her documents and performing an analysis of her circumstances, we determined that we could settle Susan's debt for a much smaller amount.

We filed for an Offer in Compromise with the IRS, and offered less than two thousand dollars in return. Knowing the IRS was owed about two hundred thousand dollars, would they agree to settle the debt for less than two thousand dollars? That would be about one cent on the dollar.

After months of negotiation, they did. With a loan from family, Susan was able to settle her IRS tax debt. She was finally able to move forward.

And, what about the State of Michigan? Likewise, we submitted an extensive amount of paperwork and were able to settle her fifteen thousand dollar tax debt for less than two hundred dollars.

Susan left our office with her head held high. She had settled a tax debt of approximately two hundred fifteen thousand dollars for a mere two thousand two hundred dollars.

Now…Susan and her children are able to move on from the wreckage of the past and start to live the life they want to lead.

CHAPTER 3
NO RECEIPTS

**Ed and Patti:
near Parchment, Michigan**

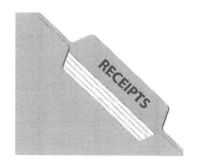

Ed worked long hours as a traveling salesman of industrial supplies. He loved getting on the road and visiting customers he had known for over twenty years.

Patti was a stay-at-home wife on disability. She was diagnosed with cancer, and she had quit her job as an assembly worker in a local factory years before. Patti often traveled with Ed just so they could spend time together.

At this point in Ed's life, he didn't need to work. But he enjoyed it. He loved getting out with Patti and visiting his customers. Besides, it was therapeutic for Patti. It gave her a reason to live.

Life was good…until a business decision by Ed's employer would turn his life upside down. There was a change in ownership in the business, and the new owner did not want employees. He only wanted independent contractors working for him. By paying Ed as an independent contractor, rather than the employee he really was, the employer did not have to pay employment taxes. It saved the employer about ten percent on his payroll taxes.

As a subcontractor, Ed now received a Form 1099 at the end of the year. This amounted to quite a change for him because it included all of the reimbursements Ed had paid out of his own pocket to pay for gas, meals and business gifts. Though on paper it looked like Ed made a lot of money, he turned around and used that same money for travel expenses and business gifts.

Ed had always prepared his own tax return, but he did not know how to do it as an independent contractor. And he didn't seek professional advice.

Ed simply did not file a tax return...for three years. And he ignored the letters from the IRS.

After four years, Ed received a visit from an IRS revenue officer. The revenue officer was friendly enough, and suggested he immediately file his tax returns so the liability would be reduced substantially.

The revenue officer said Ed would owe about thirty thousand dollars, and Ed knew that he normally received a refund as an employee.

The first step in preparing his tax returns was to get copies of his reimbursed expenses from his company. His company refused, claiming they had destroyed the receipts. Ed was confused and furious. Of course, he thought, his employer would need to keep copies for their own tax return. But they claimed not to have them.

Ed quit right then. His employer had no loyalty to the workers.

Ed knew he could find work. He had been recruited several times over the years by his company's major competitor, and all he had to do was make a phone call.

Outside of the unwanted stress on Patti, the move to the new employer was easy.

Ed's new employer made him an employee just as he should have been in his previous job. Ed knew he would no longer have problems with his tax returns in the future, but he had to deal with the past. The IRS said he owed over thirty thousand dollars.

During a visit to Patti's physician, Ed and Patti heard of me. The family physician knew me, and he referred them to me.

When Ed and Patti came to my office, I suggested we file amended tax returns. However, the problem we ran into was that Ed's previous employer said he did not have the records. I knew he did. He had to keep them for seven years in the event the business was audited by the IRS. I sent threatening letters, but short of suing the employer we would not get the records. And the IRS had no interest in sending a subpoena for them.

Ed's former employer may have had the records, but they were not about to turn them over because Ed went to work for a competitor.

We were sunk…or were we?

The IRS was pressuring us for an answer on how the tax debt would be paid, and we considered our options.

Looking at Ed's current financial condition, it was clear that we could make Ed and Patti uncollectible. In other words, the tax liability would remain but the IRS would not actively pursue the payment of that tax debt.

We considered making an installment payment plan where Ed and Patti would pay off the debt over several years. But they certainly did not have the ability to pay the IRS in addition to the crushing medical bills for Patti.

The other option we considered was preparing an Offer in Compromise because Ed and Patti could try to make the payments required. However, they had too much equity in house. They could sell the house and pay off the tax debt, but where would they live?

The best option was to make Ed and Patti uncollectible.

That's right; the IRS will not pursue a taxpayer if they are unable to pay the tax debt. There were many roadblocks that we had to get over, but since Patti had extraordinary medical expenses, we were successful. Ed and Patti qualified.

We put a stop to the IRS's collection activity and made Ed and Patti uncollectible.

Now what? Ed and Patti still owed the thirty thousand dollars, and it was only going to grow. The solution? We had Ed and Patti make sure they filed and paid their taxes going forward. We set them up so that after several years the IRS failed to pursue collection. Due to the statute of limitations, after about eight years the tax debts dropped off. It was a long road, but the taxpayers saved over thirty thousand dollars in unpaid tax debt.

Some roads take a long time to travel, but it only makes it sweeter when you cross the finish line.

CHAPTER 4
THREE MILLION DOLLAR TAX BILL

Jennifer: outside Chicago, Illinois

Jennifer had a successful business working in the health field. After only a few years she had close to a hundred employees, and the business was still growing. She had to hire more administrative staff, including an in-house accountant.

Cash flow seemed to be increasing with the new in-house accountant managing the finances. Jennifer could now afford the time to take vacations, and even bring her extended family along. It all seemed too good to be true.

It was. A dark cloud was forming.

The in-house accountant was not paying the payroll taxes. To make matters worse, the accountant hid the IRS Notices from Jennifer.

All went well for two years, but then an IRS revenue officer showed up at the door. The house of cards fell quickly.

Jennifer showed up at my door the next day, and she retained me.

My immediate concern was that this could be a criminal matter. Why would it be criminal? When an employer knowingly fails to pay over to the IRS payroll taxes withheld from an employee's payroll check, it is a criminal offense. In this case, we were talking about close to three million dollars.

Besides the criminal aspect to the case, Jennifer could also be held personally liable for part of the payroll taxes not paid over to the IRS.

I immediately talked with the IRS revenue officer, and it became clear that Jennifer never saw the IRS notices because she never saw the mail. Not a good excuse, but it was honest. My biggest concern, the criminal aspect, was taken off the table. Thank goodness.

The next issue was whether or not we could negotiate the three million dollar debt down and continue the business. This was not an option. By the time I became involved, the IRS revenue officer was upset that there was no communication for such a long period of time, and any negotiation to pay a lesser amount would only open up discussions about the criminal implications again.

Jennifer had a great reputation, but she was overwhelmed, and now felt blindsided. She was. She only wanted to stay out of jail and move on.

Jennifer decided to close the business. She had to. The debt was insurmountable. What would happen if Jennifer closed the business? Could she walk away? She could not. If she closed the business, the IRS would not pursue criminal charges but would still assess her personally for the payroll taxes withheld from the employee's paychecks but not paid to the IRS.

How much was the employee withholdings that were not paid? Just over two million dollars. So she was personally responsible for two million dollars in tax debt!

We caught a break, however. In addition to owing two million dollars in tax debt, the IRS had every reason to file a tax lien which would ruin her credit for ten years. Did they? No. The IRS understood that Jennifer was broken, both mentally and financially. There was no reason to chase her. She would never pay it off.

She also avoided jail time.

It was tough after she closed the business. She could not get a job anywhere, and she had no interest in starting a new business. She was starting her life over in another part of the State.

As the owner of the business she needed to take responsibility and check on the staff to make sure they were doing their jobs. She had failed. She had learned her lesson, but it was an expensive one that had changed her life.

It has been probably fifteen years since I dealt with this explosive IRS matter. Jennifer moved to northern Michigan, and works in the health care industry. And since IRS debts were more than ten years old, the IRS no longer sought to collect anything. (With certain exceptions, the IRS only has ten years to collect a tax debt.)

Jennifer no longer fears a knock on the door with the IRS wanting to talk with her. She loves her life now, without the responsibilities associated with owning her own business.

CHAPTER 5
ON THE STREETS

Joseph: Detroit, Michigan

Joseph was retired from the military and had found a second career as a street minister.

He and his wife had traveled the world in the military, and he often spent time with the needy. He enjoyed it, and even became a minister while still on active duty.

Now he was retired, and he had returned home to Detroit. He had seen the pain of those less fortunate throughout the world, but it was just as evident in his hometown.

Joseph soon started a ministry helping homeless vets in the city of Detroit. He loved it.

Becoming a minister was his calling, just as the military had been for twenty five years. But Joseph struggled to keep his marriage together, because his wife did not approve of his second career. Ministering on the streets of Detroit was not what she expected in retirement. She loved to travel, and Joseph was fine with her taking trips to visit relatives in her home town of Chicago.

They literally led separate lives, and it seemed to work.

One Friday night, it was time to go to work. Joseph bundled up to protect himself from the biting cold wind of the Detroit inner-city. He was off once again to shepherd, and his wife was off for another weekend trip to Chicago. And so it went. Another weekend apart.

Suddenly, Joseph fell. He fell hard. He couldn't get up. His buddies on the street hailed down a police car, and soon an ambulance arrived. Joseph had suffered a stroke, and he couldn't remember who he was or even why he was there.

Luckily, from his identification cards, it was determined that Joseph was retired military. After a visit to the emergency room, he soon found himself recovering in a bed at the local VA Hospital. His wife was located and rushed back from Chicago to be by his side. Joseph now faced a long road to recovery.

After a few weeks, Joseph was released from the hospital, but he needed bed rest to recover. His wife became his financial power of attorney, because Joseph could not handle his finances any longer. He could not even write a check. Joseph just lay in bed.

After several months, his wife became restless. This is not the retirement she had expected. Feeding and bathing her husband was not what she had signed up for. Soon she was off again on her trips, leaving Joseph for days on end at the local VA Hospital in the respite care unit.

Two years later it was over. His wife left him and filed for divorce. She moved to Chicago.

Although Joseph was now strong enough to live on his own, he found out something devastating.

Over the two year period that Joseph had turned over his finances to his wife, she had cashed in his retirement accounts as his power of attorney. Adding insult to injury, she filed her tax returns separately because Joseph owed a lot of taxes on his cashed-in retirement accounts. Joseph now owed thirty-two thousand dollars to the IRS.

In the divorce, Joseph did not want to fight his wife of thirty years. He gave her the house and did not question the cashing out of the retirement accounts. He just wanted to get back to the streets to shepherd his friends as soon as he could.

And the streets are where he ended up. He became homeless.

With his small military retirement and monthly social security income, Joseph soon found a cheap room to rent near the area where he did his ministry work. He was making it work. But soon the IRS found him.

Joseph still had not filed his tax returns for several years, but the IRS assessed him the balance due in taxes as though he had filed. The IRS levied his social security. It wasn't much, but he could not afford the one hundred and fifty-five dollars the IRS took each month from his social security payments.

Joseph found me through a referral. Someone at the VA Hospital, where he visited often for his prescriptions, knew of my office.

Joseph was hurting, and we needed to stop his pain. Joseph gave me authority to contact the IRS, and I did.

We called during his first visit to my office, and the IRS agreed to release the levy immediately. The IRS Revenue Officer on the other end of the line looked at Joseph's sources of income (yes, they have that information in the IRS computers), and determined Joseph could not pay the IRS anything.

But it didn't stop there. Our office filed an Offer in Compromise to settle the thirty two thousand tax debt once and for all. The IRS agreed to settle. We not only settled, but we settled for a mere one hundred dollars. In just three months from beginning to end, the IRS settled a thirty two thousand tax debt for one hundred dollars!

Today, Joseph is back on the streets watching his flock, exactly where he wants to be.

CHAPTER 6
LAST CALL

Sheila: near Traverse City, Michigan

A tax client of mine traveled up to Michigan's ski country for a weekend trip. He bellied up to the bar, and as often happens, bartender and patron started talking. This time, however, was different. Normally, the patron spills out his or her woes to the bartender. This time the bartender poured out her woes to the patron.

The IRS had stopped in a month ago, and they were closing the bar down for nonpayment of payroll taxes. Tax returns had not been filed for a year simply because the owner could not afford the payroll taxes.

Apparently no one was watching the books. The husband and wife team who owned the bar were having marital problems, and money came up missing. No one was watching the employees to see if they were taking from the cash register, or was it the owners taking from the till? It seemed no one was in charge, and no one wanted to deal with the IRS.

With cash flow so poor, the owners were trying to hide from the IRS by not filing their tax returns. It wasn't working.

The bar had been operating smoothly for ten years, but in the last three years everything went south.

The bartender was not painting a pretty picture. Taxes were not paid, tax forms were not filed, and the owners were running from the IRS. My client was not surprised when the bartender said the IRS was closing them down.

The bartender didn't stop there. She kept talking.

Because there was a mortgage on the operation and building, the IRS was providing the owners a way out. Sell the business, and turn over the profits. For any amounts unpaid, the owners would be personally responsible.

Because the bartender and other employees were now openly talking about the tax problem, everyone knew there was trouble with the IRS. No buyer could be found. No one was interested. It was stepping into a swamp.

This was a change from my client's normal visit to the local pub. He ordered another beer, and the bartender gave it to him on the house.

The bartender seemed to have spilled everything. What else was there to say? They stared at each other, and the patron finally felt it was time to tell his story. He was also a business owner, and though he had had tax troubles in the past, they were never quite this bad. He suggested the owner call our office. After all, we had straightened out his problem with the IRS. Maybe *Fresh Start Tax Solutions* could help with hers.

I got the call the following Monday.

The major problem was that the bar owners were simply ignoring the IRS. You can't do that. If you don't acknowledge the IRS's attempts to resolve the problem, they will enforce the collection of taxes. But be careful how you engage them, I warned. The IRS is not your friend. They will maximize taxes, interest and penalties, try to collect every dime they can get, and will not tell you how to minimize your liability.

The bar owners said that they could afford to pay the taxes, but not the penalties and interest.

We discussed the history of the tax problems and what I would do if I were in their shoes. The bar owed about thirty five thousand in unpaid taxes, and another seventeen thousand in penalties.

I had a plan…brilliant, yet simple.

I called the IRS revenue office and found that the IRS was exasperated too. The IRS wanted to help resolve the tax matter, but the bar owner was not cooperating. It was that simple. I agreed to intercede, and the IRS revenue officer agreed to work with me.

There was now open communication with the IRS, and I believed we could come to some resolution short of property seizure.

What should I ask for? I asked the IRS if we immediately filed the tax returns, could consideration be given to abating certain penalties? Agreed!

Next question…would it be acceptable to pay the taxes and interest owed over the remaining statute of limitations? Agreed!

I wish it were that simple, but this was only the beginning. We had work to do. My negotiations with the

IRS inspired the bar owner to help me in filing the tax returns. But there was still the matter of cash flow.

Were the bar owners, who were married, willing to put aside their differences and watch the cash flow? Would they watch the employees, and would they do the accounting each and every day? They agreed. Problem solved.

So a deal was worked out between the bar owners and the IRS. The actual taxes and interest due in the amount of thirty seven thousand would be paid over the next seven years, and the business would remain current in their filings. It worked. Seven years later the tax debt was paid off, and the bar is still open.

And the marriage? They are still happily married. They set aside their differences to fight the IRS, and it gave a new spark in their marriage.

Now, who do you think the bar owners gave the credit to for saving their marriage? The IRS or Fresh Start Tax Solutions LLC?

Let's just say the IRS cannot hang a shingle for marriage counseling outside their door.

CHAPTER 7
WAITED TOO LONG

**Patti and Mark:
Battle Creek, Michigan**

Patti and Mark were just leading a normal life. Mark had a factory job, and Patti worked at a retailer stocking shelves in the evening hours. They worked extra hours to put their children through college. It was a tough life at times, but rewarding.

Filing and paying their taxes had never been a problem. They had used the same tax preparer for years, and did all the right things to make sure they were not underpaid. They normally had refunds. The refunds over the last few years were larger because they received educational tax credits for the college tuition they paid for their children.

But there was a problem. They claimed too much in educational tax credits, and the IRS wanted them to pay back more than seven thousand dollars.

Patti and Mark contacted their tax preparer who only kept limited summer hours. He could meet them in a few weeks, they were told. They waited.

The IRS wanted a response in thirty days, but Patti and Mark felt comfortable the tax preparer could resolve the questions the IRS was asking. This would be quickly resolved, or so they thought.

Two weeks later they met with their tax preparer. Their hopes were immediately dashed. The tax preparer, who only worked seasonally, was unable to explain what the problem was. He could not help. In fact, it seemed he wanted nothing to do with resolving any tax problems that he may in fact have caused. He told them to just pay the tax the IRS said they owed. Patti and Mark were set adrift to resolve the tax problems themselves.

Patti called the IRS the next morning hours before work. After waiting on the telephone for over an hour, she finally reached an IRS "customer representative." She was told what the problem was, but not how to fix it other than setting up a payment plan with the IRS. All they needed was her bank account number, and they would be happy to take out one hundred fifty dollars per month for the next five years. Patti said she needed to talk with her husband first and hung up.

Patti and Mark never called back.

About forty five days later, Patti and Mark received a Final Notice from the IRS. Their options at this point were to file an Appeal within the IRS, or file in Tax Court. They called again. This time Mark was also on the phone. Again, after waiting on hold for over an hour, they were able to speak to an IRS "customer representative."

This time the IRS went into detail about what the problem was, but also gave the taxpayers an out. The agent explained that the taxpayers had taken an educational tax credit that they did not qualify for. But Patti and Mark did qualify for a smaller educational tax credit worth about one half of the one tax credit they took on their tax return. All they had to do was to file an amended tax return immediately. But they had to hurry, because they had limited time before the IRS made a final decision and would attempt to collect.

Once again, Patti and Mark could not make a decision and felt weary of signing anything with the IRS. Mark wanted to talk with the tax preparer once again so he could amend the tax return that was incorrectly filed. Patti wanted to move on and go to another tax preparer but reluctantly agreed.

Their tax preparer would not meet with them. A ten plus year relationship was over and, they were set adrift for good this time.

What would they do? They heard an "800 number" radio advertisement from a company out-of-state and called. They were told that for three thousand dollars, they would never have to hear from the IRS again. They were pleased.

But would they get out of paying the taxes? No, the sales person at the "800 number" tax resolution firm said. They would be set up on a payment plan for whatever the IRS said they owed and pay the balance owed over five years. No amended tax return would be filed. They hung up.

The next Notice received by the IRS stated that their time was up. They owed about seven thousand two hundred dollars to the IRS, and the only way to challenge it was to petition the US Tax Court.

They turned to the internet. Down the street from where they lived was *Fresh Start Tax Solutions LLC*. They called and made an appointment with our office.

Our staff went through their file and determined that the solution was straightforward. Yes, we agreed with the IRS the taxpayers took an educational tax credit on their tax return which they were not entitled to. But they were entitled to a smaller educational tax credit. We could reduce the tax liability, but Patti and Mark would have to pay the IRS something. Maybe they would pay three thousand dollars instead of seven thousand dollars.

We were able to help them, but it cost them. Instead of a simple amended tax return, we had to negotiate at length with the IRS. But even with our professional fees, they saved several thousands of dollars from what they would have paid the IRS and the "800 number" tax resolution firm. The taxpayers were pleased.

They learned that if you wait too long to reach out for help to resolve festering tax problems, they only get worse. And don't go to a seasonal tax preparer or an 800 number to solve your tax problems! Find a competent tax professional who is local!

CHAPTER 8
SLAMMING ON
THE BRAKES

Rick: near Baldwin, Michigan

Rick was a long haul truck driver. He was paid by the mile and was typically on the road a week at a time before returning to his wife and little girl for a few days. Rick was an immigrant and prided himself on living the American dream. He was able to buy a tractor, and he ran loads from Michigan to various places all around the country. He was able to purchase a small home and support his wife and daughter.

In January 2009, Rick was in an accident and his truck was totaled. It was a setback, but Rick was not hurt, and he had insurance. He was able to purchase a used tractor and was back on the road after a month.

But Rick lost more than truck. He lost his accounting records that he meticulously kept. They were scattered across the snowy fields of Iowa.

So Rick failed to file his 2008 tax return.

Rick started keeping his records again, but he failed to file 2009 and 2010 tax returns as well. Unsure of what to do, he was sticking his head in the sand.

By now Rick was getting letters from the IRS. They were threatening to seize his income. Now he was scared.

While driving cross country, Rick listened to a lot of radio. Every ten minutes, it seemed, there was an "800 number" tax resolution company urging him to CALL NOW! He had nowhere to turn. He needed help, so he called.

The salesman on the other end was convincing. Rick was told he would never be harassed by the IRS again if he just signed a power of attorney and provided them with his credit card information. He did, and he paid the company four thousand dollars.

Over the next month, the "800 number" tax resolution company prepared and filed the three years of missing tax returns. But the tax returns indicated he now owed sixty five thousand dollars. And they sent him paperwork to enter into a rather large monthly payment to the IRS.

He was confused. Why sixty five thousand dollars for three years of taxes? That was an average of over twenty thousand dollars per year!

In the past, when Rick prepared his own tax returns, he normally paid about eight thousand in taxes per year, but never twenty thousand dollars per year!

The "800 number" national tax resolution firm continued to pressure Rick to sign an installment agreement with the IRS for over thirteen hundred dollars per month, so he did. What choice did he have?

The "800 number" national tax resolution firm disappeared as quickly as they came into his life.

The monthly payments were crushing, and Rick's business and marriage were suffering. He could not continue paying and started to default after a few months. The IRS started to send more letters, and this time they were getting very aggressive. Now he had less than thirty days before the IRS would levy his only source of income.

While in a truck stop in Indiana, another trucker, whom I had helped out years earlier, heard Rick's story. He told Rick to call our office for a second opinion.

Rick called me when he was on the road traveling back home, and we arranged a time to meet the next day.

While Rick was at my office, I called the IRS and received an electronic copy of his tax returns for the three years the "800 number" tax resolution prepared them. What we found was explosive!

The tax preparer had not taken any business expenses on the tax returns! With any business, and especially trucking, you have expenses. Over-the-road self-employed truck drivers normally have fuel and repair expenses. Also, they're allowed expenses for hotel and food. The "800 number" national tax resolution firm was in such a hurry to push the case through to maximize their own profits, they had failed to deduct any of Rick's business expenses.

Rick immediately knew this was the cause of the inflated tax liabilities for the years the "800 number" tax resolution firm filed the tax returns. Rick had provided the "800 number" tax resolution firm the expense information, but they had never bothered to use it on the tax returns to reduce the taxable income!

I told Rick we could help. I didn't know the extent to which we could help, but we could help. There were a lot of issues to review, including whether or not it was too late to file amended tax returns.

Over the next several weeks we gathered the missing information for 2009 and 2010. Luckily, Rick kept detailed copies of the information he had sent to the "800 number" tax resolution firm to prepare those tax returns.

The year 2008 was a different animal. Rick did not have records. They were lost in the February 2009 tractor accident. We decided to estimate that year based upon Rick's extensive records for the other years.

After amending the tax returns to include Rick's business expenses, the tax liability for 2008, 2009 and 2010 was now a more reasonable twenty-four thousand, with an additional three thousand in penalties and interest. This was a far cry from the sixty-five thousand the "800 number" tax resolution prepared.

There were a few ways we could approach the IRS on this case, but the cheapest route in terms of professional fees was to have Rick amend his tax returns and submit them to the IRS to see if they would accept them after this late date. We took a chance and filed the amended tax returns.

While I filed paperwork to the IRS Appeal Division to delay any collection activity, the IRS processed and approved of the changes we requested. The IRS accepted a reduction of tax liabilities of approximately sixty-five thousand down to twenty-seven thousand, which again included the interest and penalties.

We were able to abate some penalties, which further reduced the liability one thousand dollars. All told, our firm was able to reduce the tax liability by forty thousand dollars.

The next step was how to pay this liability. We looked at several ways, but we ended up setting up a payment plan just as the "800 number" tax resolution firm had done. However, instead of over thirteen hundred dollars a month, we were able to settle on five hundred dollars per month.

Rick found it amazing that he provided the same information to two different tax resolution firms (one local and one national) with such dramatically different results. I wasn't.

CHAPTER 9
WRECKAGE FROM THE PAST

Chad and Lisa:
Fowlerville, Michigan

How often is it that you want to do something, but you're scared to take that step because you have some wreckage from the past that has not been resolved?

Chad and Lisa had been dating for about two years. She had two small children from a previous marriage.

They talked of marriage, but Chad balked. Was it the children? "Absolutely not," Chad told her.

Chad had a secret.

Chad finally admitted to Lisa that he had not filed taxes for several years and didn't want to drag her and the children into his mess.

Lisa asked for permission to reach out and seek help. He eagerly agreed. He wanted the pain to go away and appreciated that Lisa offered to help.

Lisa knew Chad was frozen in fear. She looked on the internet and quickly found my website, *FreshStartTaxSolutions.com*. We were local to Michigan. She called, and we talked. We could help.

Chad came in a few days later.

Chad admitted he had a tax problem and had just ignored the IRS. He had received letters, but he was self-employed with no bank account. Could the IRS really find him? He hoped not. I told him that was mostly true…for now. But what if Chad ever wanted to retire? They would levy his social security. What if he wanted to buy a house? They would put a lien on the house so that he could not build any equity in it. What if Lisa's children wanted to go to college? He would have to provide a tax return for any scholarships.

Chad had a mess. Wreckage.

I got right to work, and we reviewed Chad's finances. After analyzing everything, I told Chad what he already knew. He had a substantial tax liability. Based on the information provided, I calculated the tax debt would be approximately fifty six thousand dollars over four years. He would also owe the State of Michigan.

Chad handed over his IRS Notices. There were several. I reviewed them and mentioned I thought there were several more that he had not received over the past twelve months because he had moved, and the IRS did not have his current address. This was more uncertainty about where Chad stood with the IRS.

Chad had a decision to make. Did he continue running, maybe even leaving Lisa and the children he had come to love? Or did he face his fears and deal with the IRS and State of Michigan head-on?

He decided to let *Fresh Start Tax Solutions* take on the IRS and State.

We got to work.

Our first objective was to prepare the missing, unfiled tax returns. We had little information as Chad did not keep his records nor did he have a bank account. I explained to Chad that we wanted to prepare accurate tax returns, but if we lacked information we should make reasonable estimates. I also had to disclose this on the tax return I was filing. Chad understood. So, based upon industry standards, we estimated what we thought was a reasonable income and expenses for the four years he had not filed.

Once we prepared the tax returns, we had to determine how we would approach the IRS after they were filed and the taxes assessed. Chad could not afford a rather large installment agreement. Fortunately he qualified for an Offer in Compromise, since he did not have many assets.

We filed the tax returns, and shortly thereafter filed an Offer in Compromise with the IRS to settle the debt for what he could afford.

After haggling with the IRS because they wanted more documentation, we finally settled the total tax debt for about eight thousand dollars. Chad had to pay this under certain guidelines established by the IRS. He accepted the IRS offer to settle. He was pleased. He settled a fifty six thousand dollar tax debt for eight thousand dollars!

But we were not done. The State of Michigan was now getting very aggressive.

The State of Michigan follows its own rules that are specific to the State. (Frankly, many national "800 number" tax resolution firms either ignore the State side of a tax controversy, or they don't have the expertise in the state law.)

We also filed an Offer with the State, and settled that debt for about fourteen cents on the dollar. Chad borrowed the money for the State and paid them immediately.

Chad's wreckage of the past was now just that…in the past. He could move on with his life.

Needless to say, Chad and Lisa are now married. They have their home, and a third child on the way.

CHAPTER 10
THE IRS BULLY

Max and Cindy: Bangor, Maine

This is an old case of mine dating back to the 90's. Those were the days when the IRS was out of control. In those days, home seizures were a game to the IRS. In fact, in the Oklahoma City IRS office, the agents were having contests to see who could seize more taxpayer residences. Hopefully, those days are over forever. The IRS claims to have cleansed itself and set up new procedures for seizing assets. The IRS can still seize residences, but these days it's rare.

This case started when I received a call from a psychiatrist working at a State hospital. This doctor dealt with some of the worst psychological cases imaginable, but he couldn't conceive how to respond to what the IRS was doing to him and his wife now.

Max had been in private practice and was a few years behind in taxes. He made estimated tax payments, but he just couldn't seem to keep up. Max was an excellent doctor, but not a very good business person. So he closed his business and took a position with the State of Maine. His new position involved visiting several hospitals throughout the State, and he wasn't home often.

During this transition from self-employment to working as an employee, Max called the IRS and asked for help in setting up a payment plan for his past tax debt. The IRS told him they would assign a revenue officer to talk with him. He was looking forward to working out a payment plan and getting into the good graces with the IRS once again.

What happened next is something no family should endure.

While Max was traveling on business and away from home, an IRS revenue officer visited the residence. The revenue officer wanted to come in and talk. Cindy normally did not allow strangers in the house, especially with her husband's line of business. But Cindy knew he had contacted the IRS, and they were expecting a phone call. This was a knock on the door, however. But the revenue officer was a woman. What could go wrong? Although apprehensive, Cindy let the IRS agent in.

Once in the house, the revenue officer made Cindy feel like a criminal. The revenue officer immediately started pointing at the paintings on the walls, the furniture, and other valuables. The revenue officer told Cindy the IRS would seize the personal belongings and sell them. Then she left, leaving behind a demand letter for immediate full payment.

When Max returned a day later, he found his wife in bed crying hysterically. She was having a nervous breakdown.

Cindy had fragile nerves, and Max did all he could do to protect her. But this unwarranted confrontation was over the top, for anyone. Now Max was faced with putting his own wife in the hospital where he worked.

Like many of my clients, Max heard about me by word of mouth.

He called, and we talked. A few days later, Max and Cindy drove to my office so I could hear Cindy's side of the story.

I listened, and was stunned. This taxpayer only needed a simple installment agreement, but was bullied by a rogue revenue officer who apparently did not appreciate being assigned the case. She was a revenue officer with a huge ego and no empathy. This revenue officer apparently liked to bully anyone that did not shake in their boots at the mere mention of her name.

I was angry, but this was an easy fix. I would simply call the revenue officer's manager and ask to be assigned to another revenue officer. Then we would set up an installment agreement with a new revenue officer.

But Cindy balked. She was still deathly afraid of the bully. Max mentioned this was a common response by those who had experienced a psychological episode such as Cindy's. "Just give her whatever she wants!" Cindy pleaded.

Max shrugged. "Let's get this done as soon as humanly possible so we can get on with our lives," he said. I was ready for battle, but Max told me to just capitulate to the bully.

Max owed approximately twenty thousand dollars and could pay off the debt in a year with his new job. And, if needed, he could mortgage the house to have it paid off sooner. I understood my client's wishes. Just get the IRS out of their lives!

I prepared the powers of attorney so that I could talk with the revenue officer. I also provided terms of repayment that the IRS had to accept. The debt would be paid off in less than a year, with full payment of interest and penalties.

The IRS accepted it, and the case was closed. I would never have my revenge. Or would I?

About six months later, news of IRS abuses nationwide started to surface in the media. It appeared this was a concerted effort by the IRS to intimidate taxpayers. Already in the news there were reports of rogue IRS agents, but now Congress was starting to investigate.

The bully behavior of the IRS started to make sense to me now. Right before this incident, another revenue officer who I worked with regularly abruptly announced he was quitting the IRS. I asked him why. His response was simply that he could not morally do what he was being asked to do. His comment did not register with me at the time. But now, with the Congressional hearings, it certainly made sense. There was an ongoing effort to intimidate taxpayers, and the bullies at the IRS thrived.

My friend, the revenue officer, did not want to work in that environment. So he quit.

With the news of IRS abuses, Congress called the ROTH hearings. They asked tax professionals to send any of their cases involving abuse of power by the IRS.

You can bet that this case was reported to Congress in a New York minute.

My advice? Don't enter into a payment plan with the IRS by yourself, because there is always a chance you'll run into that schoolyard bully.

CHAPTER 11
FIRE THAT SOB!

Rose, Lewiston, Maine

This is another horror story with the IRS that actually ended quite nicely.

This case started out as a simple theft by an IRS revenue officer. My client, Rose, owned a small bed and breakfast/gift shop in Ogunquit, Maine. She had a visitor over a summer weekend. This visitor made it very clear she was an IRS revenue officer and asked for special favors throughout the weekend. My client was fine with that. She had a lot of quirky customers, and this one fit the bill.

But there was a twist. The revenue officer bounced a twenty dollar check, and she refused to pay when Rose contacted her weeks later. My client felt bullied. Normally she would write it off, but the revenue officer was so abusive during her stay that she wanted to pursue collection action.

Rose asked me if here was anything I could do, and I thought about it. She could turn this person into the police, but that would mean making a sworn statement, taking time out of her day, and maybe even going to court. No, she just wanted to be paid and not harm the quirky customer.

Since the IRS revenue officer made a show of the fact she wielded so much power, I figured just calling her manager would keep this issue from getting out of hand. I knew how to deal with bullies. I called her manager. I explained to the manager that my client did not want trouble. However, one of his revenue officers was clearing abusing her authority, telling a shopkeeper she was an IRS revenue officer, bouncing a check, and then refusing to honor it.

A new check arrived the following week, and it cleared this time. Case closed. Or was it?

About three months later, I received a referral from a real estate broker about someone who was being bullied by a woman revenue officer. Who could it be? Maine was not that big in terms of population, and I only knew of two women revenue officers. In my book they were both bullies. Which one this time, I wondered?

I signed the power of attorney and faxed it in. I followed up a week later, and the revenue officer answered. I thought we could settle the matter on the phone, but she felt otherwise. She wanted me to drive three hours one way to her office in Bangor, Maine. I could have bounced the case up to the manager, but I didn't. I wanted to meet this bully anyway, and this was my chance.

So a few weeks later I drove to Bangor to meet the IRS revenue officer. This was the same one that tried to stiff the shopkeeper client of mine. I was prepared to settle the matter with all of the paperwork required to complete an installment agreement.

But the revenue officer was not there. She was at my client's office three hours away. We had crossed paths.

I was being played, and I didn't like it. First, the revenue officer misled me as to where the meeting was to take place. Second, the revenue officer was talking to my client without me being present. This second matter was a clear violation of IRS policy.

This was before the days of cell phones, and I did not find out about this until a few days later. I tried to call the IRS revenue officer to re-schedule, but to no avail. I also tried to call my client, also to no avail.

My referral, the real estate broker, finally called me and told me what had happened. The revenue officer had tracked Rose down at a bowling alley where she worked. She told Rose in no uncertain terms that "Chris Micklatcher is a SOB, and I will not deal with him." The revenue officer told my client to "fire Chris Micklatcher." In return, the IRS revenue officer would give Rose a "sweet deal." So they settled.

I immediately called the IRS manager to complain about the revenue officer's behavior. I admitted my client got a sweet deal, so the manager and I agreed to drop my complaint. If I wanted, the manager said, he could have the case reassigned and opened again. Neither my client nor I wanted to let this "sweet deal" go. So we let the matter drop.

Right then I realized two things. First, the reputation of some IRS revenue officers is richly deserved. Second, the IRS protects their own.

The vast majority of IRS agents I deal with are reputable. But a few bad apples can spoil the whole bunch.

CHAPTER 12
A FRESH START

mistake

Jacob: Battle Creek, Michigan

One of my first clients after moving into my new office was Jacob. He was a young guy of about eighty-five. He had a problem with his tax return, and he simply could not believe that he owed the seventeen thousand that the IRS said he did. He even went to a "800 number" tax resolution firm, who insisted the amount was correct, and they could set him up in an installment payment plan for about four hundred dollars a month for five years.

He was frustrated. He wanted a second opinion.

Jacob found me like most of my clients do. He was a referral.

Jacob sat down and got right to the point. He explained that the tax preparer simply got the tax return wrong. Jacob rolled over a retirement plan from one trustee to another. He did not take an IRA distribution. He insisted there was no tax due!

But the IRS and the "800 number" tax resolution firm both thought differently. They thought he owed.

I asked him to prove he was right, and that the IRS was wrong.

He was prepared.

Jacob pulled the documents to prove his point. Lo and behold, he was right. In fact, it was quite obvious to me.

It was also obvious to me that the tax resolution firm would not get paid if Jacob did not need their services.

I had Jacob sign a power of attorney, and we called the IRS. I explained that the original tax return was simply incorrectly prepared, and that he owed nothing to the IRS.

By now, Jacob had been in my office for about an hour. After about ten minutes I was connected to an IRS revenue officer, and we discussed what I thought was an incorrectly filed tax return. The revenue officer asked me to fax the information to her and she reviewed the documentation.

She agreed with Jacob. He did not owe anything.

In less than two hours we were able to close the case on Jacob and save him seventeen thousand dollars in taxes.

As Jacob was packing up his files to leave, he turned and faced me. He was hunched over, leaning on his cane. He was frail, but full of spunk.

He told me that I had given him a *fresh start* in life.

We both laughed. Jacob was eighty five. But he left the office with a little more pep in his step.

I was thinking of changing my company's name since we had just moved. So, a week later, in honor of Jacob, I changed it to *Fresh Start Tax Solutions*.

CHAPTER 13
WHAT'S YOUR FIRST STEP?

In the previous chapters, I discussed some of my hundreds of tax resolution cases. These are but a sample, and I tried to provide a wide variety of cases.

My hope is that you seek the advice of a tax professional. But who should you contact? We are all bombarded by the television and radio ads from the "800 numbers".

I'll bet there is someone local you can contact, and not one of those "800 number" companies.

Why contact someone locally? First, they exist. Second, they most likely have a prior history with the revenue officer or agent you are dealing with. Third, they know your state and local tax laws too. If you have an IRS problem, chances are you have a state or local tax law problem too.

If you do call an "800 number," just remember they work on volume. They treat everyone the same, and you end up paying for it. Maybe you have a twist in your personal story that only a local tax resolution specialist can understand and explain to an IRS agent. I do this regularly.

The "800 number's" business model is pushing cases through, collecting the fee, and closing them rapidly. As a result, you may have left thousands of dollars on the table.

Think of Rick, the long-haul trucker. You may initially applaud the 800 number for their swiftness in entering into an installment agreement with the IRS, but you lost in the end! And the sad part is that you never knew it.

It's important to understand that every case is unique, and the solution to your case depends on your particular facts and circumstances. Don't allow yourself to be treated like a commodity and put into a box.

It's also important to know that you have a local tax resolution expert who understands your geographical facts and circumstances. Me? Though I have clients from around the country and also assist other practitioners across the country with their more troubling cases, I concentrate my practice on Michigan cases. Sure, the IRS is national in scope, and I can work cases anywhere (and I do), but I want to keep my caseload manageable, and local to Michigan. Remember, if you have an IRS problem, you most likely also have a State of Michigan tax problem. Who better to solve a state tax problem than a local professional in your state?

Why do I tell you this? My hope is that you find a local company that specializes in tax resolution, not a national mill. You'll get the best deal with the IRS this way.

Where should you go if you have a problem with the IRS? If you have a problem with the IRS, give our office a call at 269-969-9752. Alternatively, connect with us through our website at *freshstarttaxsolutions.com*.

Where should you go if you have a problem with the State you live in? Again, give our office a call at 269-969-9752. Alternatively, connect with us through our website at *freshstarttaxsolutions.com.* If you need help with a particular State and we don't support that State, I will locate a competent professional in that State for you! I work with local professionals throughout the United States.

CONCLUSION

I wonder if you heard your story in these pages? If not, I have more stories…many more.

My purpose in writing this book is two-fold.

First, I don't want you to be so afraid of the IRS that you are frozen into inaction. Get help! Take action now!

Second, I want to encourage you to find someone local, in your state, to resolve your tax problems. Take my suggestions in the final chapter of the book where I explain how to get local, competent help.

Take the next step and call for help. I, along with our team of tax professionals in our office, take a limited number of new tax resolution cases each month. If you would like to speak with me, or a member of our team, call us at 269-969-9752. Our web address is http://freshstarttaxsolutions.com

The wilderness you find yourself in is simply
the road between the wreckage of the past
and the life you want to lead.
You only need to stop, and ask for directions.

—Chris Micklatcher

51761866R00040

Made in the USA
Middletown, DE
04 July 2019